"Dear little Swallow," said the Prince, "you tell me of marvelous things,

but more marvelous than anything is the suffering of men and of women."

CREATIVE SHORT STORIES

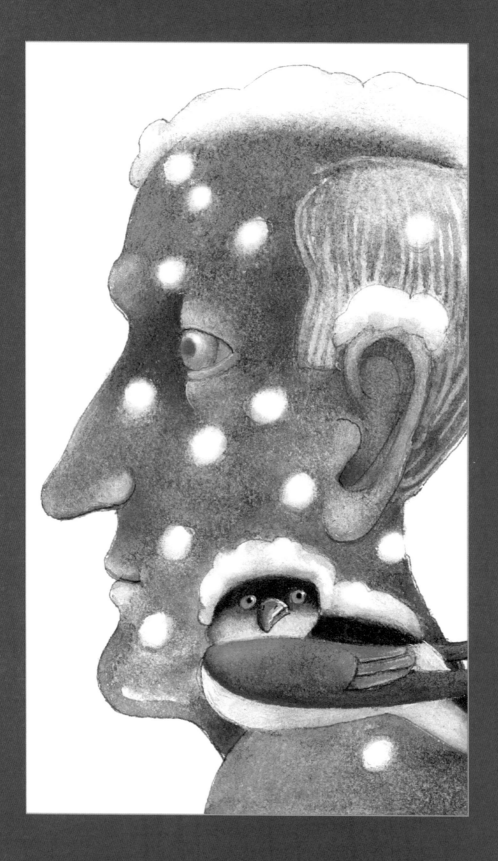

THE HAPPY PRINCE

OSCAR WILDE

CREATIVE EDUCATION

High above the city, on a tall column, stood the statue of the Happy Prince. He was gilded all over with thin leaves of fine gold, for eyes he had two bright sapphires, and a large red ruby glowed on his sword hilt.

He was very much admired indeed. "He is as beautiful as a weathercock," remarked one of the Town Councillors who wished to gain a reputation for having artistic tastes; "only not quite so useful," he added, fearing lest people should think him unpractical, which he really was not.

"Why can't you be like the Happy Prince?" asked a sensible mother of her little boy who was crying for the moon. "The Happy Prince never dreams of crying for anything."

"I am glad there is someone in the world who is quite happy," muttered a disappointed man as he gazed at the wonderful statue.

"He looks just like an angel," said the Charity Children as they came out of the cathedral in their bright scarlet cloaks and their clean white pinafores.

"How do you know?" said the Mathematical Master. "You have never seen one."

"Ah! but we have, in our dreams," answered the children; and the Mathematical Master frowned and looked very severe, for he did not approve of children dreaming.

One night there flew over the city a little Swallow. His friends had gone away to Egypt six weeks before, but he had stayed behind, for he was in love with the most beautiful Reed. He had met her early in the spring as he was flying down the river after a big yellow moth, and had been so attracted by her slender waist that he had stopped to talk to her.

"Shall I love you?" said the Swallow, who liked to come to the point at once, and the Reed made him a low bow. So he flew round and round her, touching the water with his wings, and making silver ripples. This was his courtship, and it lasted all through the summer.

"It is a ridiculous attachment," twittered the other Swallows; "she has no money, and far too many relations"; and indeed the river was quite full of Reeds. Then, when the autumn came they all flew away.

After they had gone he felt lonely, and began to tire of his ladylove. "She has no conversation," he said, "and I am afraid that she is a coquette, for she is always flirting with the wind." And certainly, whenever the wind blew, the Reed made the most graceful curtsies. "I admit that she is domestic," he continued, "but I love traveling, and my wife, consequently, should love traveling also."

"Will you come away with me?" he said finally to her, but the Reed shook her head, she was so attached to her home.

"You have been trifling with me," he cried. "I am off to the Pyramids. Good-bye!" and he flew away.

All day long he flew, and at nighttime he arrived at the city. "Where shall I put up?" he said; "I hope the town has made preparations."

Then he saw the statue on the tall column.

"I will put up there," he cried; "it is a fine position, with plenty of fresh air." So he alighted just between the feet of the Happy Prince.

"I have a golden bedroom," he said softly to himself as he looked round, and he prepared to go to sleep; but just as he was putting his head under his wing a large drop of water fell on him.

"What a curious thing!" he cried; "there is not a single cloud in the sky, the stars are quite clear and bright, and yet it is raining. The climate in the north of Europe is really dreadful. The Reed used to like the rain, but that was merely her selfishness."

Then another drop fell.

"What is the use of a statue if it cannot keep the rain off?" he said; "I must look for a good chimney pot," and he determined to fly away.

But before he had opened his wings, a third drop fell, and he looked up, and saw—Ah! what did he see?

The eyes of the Happy Prince were filled with tears, and tears were running down his golden cheeks. His face was so beautiful in the moonlight that the little Swallow was filled with pity.

"Who are you?" he said.

"I am the Happy Prince."

"Why are you weeping then?" asked the Swallow; "you have quite drenched me."

"When I was alive and had a human heart," answered the statue, "I did not know what tears were, for I lived in the Palace of Sans-Souci, where sorrow is not allowed to enter. In the daytime I played with my companions in the garden, and in the evening I led the dance in the Great Hall. Round the garden ran a very lofty wall, but I never cared to ask what lay beyond it, everything about me was so beautiful. My courtiers called me the Happy Prince, and happy indeed I was, if pleasure be happiness. So I lived, and so I died. And now that I am dead they have set me up here so high that I can see all the ugliness and all the misery of my city, and though my heart is made of lead yet I cannot choose but weep."

"What! is he not solid gold?" said the Swallow to himself. He was too polite to make any personal remarks out loud.

"Far away," continued the statue in a low musical voice, "far away in a little street there is a poor house. One of the windows is open, and through it I can see a woman seated at a table. Her face is thin and worn, and she has coarse, red hands, all pricked by the needle, for she is a seamstress. She is embroidering passionflowers on a satin gown for the loveliest of the Queen's maids of honor to wear at the next Court ball. In a bed in the corner of the room her little boy is lying ill. He has a fever, and is asking for oranges. His mother has nothing to give him but river water, so he is crying. Swallow, Swallow, little Swallow, will you not bring her the ruby out of my sword hilt? My feet are fastened to this pedestal and I cannot move."

"I am waited for in Egypt," said the Swallow. "My friends are flying up and down the Nile, and talking to the large lotus flowers. Soon they will go to sleep in the tomb of the great King. The King is there himself in his painted coffin. He is wrapped in yellow linen, and embalmed with spices. Round his neck is a chain of pale green jade, and his hands are like withered leaves."

"Swallow, Swallow, little Swallow," said the Prince, "will you not stay with me for one night, and be my messenger? The boy is so thirsty, and the mother so sad."

"I don't think I like boys," answered the Swallow. "Last summer, when I was staying on the river, there were two rude boys, the miller's sons, who were always throwing stones at me. They never hit me, of course; we swallows fly far too well for that, and besides, I come of a family famous for its agility; but still, it was a mark of disrespect."

But the Happy Prince looked so sad that the little Swallow was sorry. "It is very cold here," he said; "but I will stay with you for one night, and be your messenger."

"Thank you, little Swallow," said the Prince.

So the Swallow picked out the great ruby from the Prince's sword, and flew away with it in his beak over the roofs of the town.

He passed by the cathedral tower, where the white marble angels were sculptured. He passed by the palace and heard the sound of dancing.

A beautiful girl came out on the balcony with her lover. "How wonderful the stars are," he said to her, "and how wonderful is the power of love!"

"I hope my dress will be ready in time for the State ball," she answered; "I have ordered passionflowers to be embroidered on it: but the seamstresses are so lazy."

He passed over the river, and saw the lanterns hanging to the masts of the ships. He passed over the Ghetto, and saw the old Jews bargaining with each other, and weighing out money in copper scales. At last he came to the poor house and looked in. The boy was tossing feverishly on his bed, and the mother had fallen asleep, she was so tired. In he hopped, and laid the great ruby on the table beside the woman's thimble. Then he flew gently round the bed, fanning the boy's forehead with his wings. "How cool I feel," said the boy, "I must be getting better"; and he sank into a delicious slumber.

Then the Swallow flew back to the Happy Prince, and told him what he had done. "It is curious," he remarked, "but I feel quite warm now, although it is so cold."

"That is because you have done a good action," said the Prince. And the little Swallow began to think, and then he fell asleep. Thinking always made him sleepy.

When day broke he flew down to the river and had a bath. "What a remarkable phenomenon," said the Professor of Ornithology as he was passing over the bridge. "A swallow in winter!" And he wrote a long letter about it to the local newspaper. Everyone quoted it, it was full of so many words that they could not understand.

"Tonight I go to Egypt," said the Swallow, and he was in high spirits at the prospect. He visited all the public monuments, and sat a long time on top of the church steeple. Wherever he went the Sparrows chirruped, and said to each other, "What a distinguished stranger!" so he enjoyed himself very much.

When the moon rose he flew back to the Happy Prince. "Have you any commissions for Egypt?" he cried; "I am just starting."

"Swallow, Swallow, little Swallow," said the Prince, "will you not stay with me one night longer?"

"I am waited for in Egypt," answered the Swallow. "Tomorrow my friends will fly up to the Second Cataract. The river horse couches there among the bulrushes, and on a great granite throne sits the God Memnon. All night long he watches the stars, and when the morning star shines he utters one cry of joy, and then he is silent. At noon the yellow lions come down to the water's edge to drink. They have eyes like green beryls, and their roar is louder than the roar of the cataract."

"Swallow, Swallow, little Swallow," said the Prince, "far away across the city I see a young man in a garret. He is leaning over a desk covered with papers, and in a tumbler by his side there is a bunch of withered violets. His hair is brown and crisp, and his lips are red as a pomegranate, and he has large and dreamy eyes. He is trying to finish a play for the Director of the Theatre, but he is too cold to write anymore. There is no fire in the grate, and hunger has made him faint."

"I will wait with you one night longer," said the Swallow, who really had a good heart. "Shall I take him another ruby?"

"Alas! I have no ruby now," said the Prince: "my eyes are all that I have left. They are made of rare sapphires, which were brought out of India a thousand years ago. Pluck out one of them and take it to him. He will sell it to the jeweler, and buy firewood, and finish his play."

"Dear Prince," said the Swallow, "I cannot do that"; and he began to weep.

"Swallow, Swallow, little Swallow," said the Prince, "do as I command you."

So the Swallow plucked out the Prince's eye, and flew away to the student's garret. It was easy enough to get in, as there was a hole in the roof. Through this he darted, and came into the room. The young man had his head buried in his hands, so he did not hear the flutter of the bird's wings, and when he looked up he found the beautiful sapphire lying on the withered violets.

"I am beginning to be appreciated," he cried; "this is from some great admirer. Now I can finish my play," and he looked quite happy.

The next day the Swallow flew down to the harbor. He sat on the mast of a large vessel and watched the sailors hauling big chests out of the hold with ropes. "Heave ahoy!" they shouted as each chest came up. "I am going to Egypt!" cried the Swallow, but nobody minded, and when the moon rose he flew back to the Happy Prince.

"I am come to bid you good-bye," he cried.

"Swallow, Swallow, little Swallow," said the Prince, "will you not stay with me one night longer?"

"It is winter," answered the Swallow, "and the chill snow will soon be here. In Egypt the sun is warm on the green palm trees, and the crocodiles lie in the mud and look lazily about them. My companions are building a nest in the Temple of Baalbec, and the pink and white doves are watching them, and cooing to each other. Dear Prince, I must leave you, but I will never forget you, and next spring I will bring you back two beautiful jewels in place of those you have given away. The ruby shall be redder than a red rose, and the sapphire shall be as blue as the great sea."

"In the square below," said the Happy Prince, "there stands a little match girl. She has let her matches fall in the gutter, and they are all spoiled. Her father will beat her if she does not bring home some money, and she is crying. She has no shoes or stockings, and her little head is bare. Pluck out my other eye, and give it to her, and her father will not beat her."

"I will stay with you one night longer," said the Swallow, "but I cannot pluck out your eye. You would be quite blind then."

"Swallow, Swallow, little Swallow," said the Prince, "do as I command you."

So he plucked out the Prince's other eye, and darted down with it. He swooped past the match girl, and slipped the jewel into the palm of her hand. "What a lovely bit of glass," cried the little girl; and she ran home, laughing.

Then the Swallow came back to the Prince. "You are blind now," he said, "so I will stay with you always."

"No, little Swallow," said the poor Prince, "you must go away to Egypt."

"I will stay with you always," said the Swallow, and he slept at the Prince's feet.

All the next day he sat on the Prince's shoulder, and told him stories of what he had seen in strange lands. He told him of the red ibises, who stand in long rows on the banks of the Nile, and catch goldfish in their beaks; of the Sphinx, who is as old as the world itself, and lives in the desert, and knows everything; of the merchants, who walk slowly by the side of their camels and carry amber beads in their hands; of the King of the Mountains of the Moon, who is as black as ebony, and worships a large crystal; of the great green snake that sleeps in a palm tree, and has twenty priests to feed it with honey cakes; and of the pygmies who sail over a big lake on large flat leaves, and are always at war with the butterflies.

"Dear little Swallow," said the Prince, "you tell me of marvelous things, but more marvelous than anything is the suffering of men and of women. There is no Mystery so great as Misery. Fly over my city, little Swallow, and tell me what you see there."

So the Swallow flew over the great city, and saw the rich making merry in their beautiful houses, while the beggars were sitting at the gates. He flew into dark lanes, and saw the white faces of starving children looking out listlessly at the black streets. Under the archway of a bridge two little boys were lying in one another's arms to try and keep themselves warm. "How hungry we are!" they said. "You must not lie here," shouted the watchman, and they wandered out into the rain.

Then he flew back and told the Prince what he had seen.

"I am covered with fine gold," said the Prince, "you must take it off, leaf by leaf, and give it to my poor; the living always think that gold can make them happy."

Leaf after leaf of the fine gold the Swallow picked off, till the Happy Prince looked quite dull and gray. Leaf after leaf of the fine gold he brought to the poor, and the children's faces grew rosier, and they laughed and played games in the street. "We have bread now!" they cried.

Then the snow came, and after the snow came the frost. The

streets looked as if they were made of silver, they were so bright and glistening; long icicles like crystal daggers hung down from the eaves of the houses, everybody went about in furs, and the little boys wore scarlet caps and skated on the ice.

The poor little Swallow grew colder and colder, but he would not leave the Prince, he loved him too well. He picked up crumbs outside the baker's door when the baker was not looking, and tried to keep himself warm by flapping his wings.

But at last he knew that he was going to die. He had just enough strength to fly up to the Prince's shoulder once more. "Good-bye, dear Prince!" he murmured, "will you let me kiss your hand?"

"I am glad that you are going to Egypt at last, little Swallow," said the Prince, "you have stayed too long here; but you must kiss me on the lips, for I love you."

"It is not to Egypt that I am going," said the Swallow. "I am going to the House of Death. Death is the brother of Sleep, is he not?"

And he kissed the Happy Prince on the lips, and fell down dead at his feet.

At that moment a curious crack sounded inside the statue, as if something had broken. The fact is that the leaden heart had snapped right in two. It certainly was a dreadfully hard frost.

Early the next morning the Mayor was walking in the square below in company with the Town Councillors. As they passed the column he looked up at the statue: "Dear me! how shabby the Happy Prince looks!" he said.

"How shabby indeed!" cried the Town Councillors, who always agreed with the Mayor; and they went up to look at it.

"The ruby has fallen out of his sword, his eyes are gone, and he is golden no longer," said the Mayor; "in fact, he is little better than a beggar!"

"Little better than a beggar," said the Town Councillors.

"And here is actually a dead bird at his feet!" continued the Mayor. "We must really issue a proclamation that birds are not to be allowed to die here." And the Town Clerk made a note of the suggestion.

So they pulled down the statue of the Happy Prince. "As he is no longer beautiful he is no longer useful," said the Art Professor at the University.

Then they melted the statue in a furnace, and the Mayor held a meeting of the Corporation to decide what was to be done with the metal.

"We must have another statue, of course," he said, "and it shall be a statue of myself."

"Of myself," said each of the Town Councillors, and they quarreled. When I last heard of them they were quarreling still.

"What a strange thing!" said the overseer of the workmen at the foundry. "This broken lead heart will not melt in the furnace. We must throw it away." So they threw it on a dust heap where the dead Swallow was also lying.

"Bring me the two most precious things in the city," said God to one of His Angels; and the Angel brought Him the leaden heart and the dead bird.

"You have rightly chosen," said God, "for in my garden of Paradise this little bird shall sing forevermore, and in my city of gold the Happy Prince shall praise me."

In the last half of the 19th century, a new artistic and literary movement took hold in British culture. It was called aestheticism, and it placed a priority on beauty, insisting that life should imitate art and strive to be as beautiful as artwork. Aestheticism also dictated that art should be created for art's sake only, not for commercial purposes or to advance certain ideas. Oscar Wilde was one of the movement's flashiest proponents and promoted himself as a devoted aesthete long before he contributed any literary art to the movement. His fairy tale "The Happy Prince" is one of the best examples of his aesthetic values and, at the same time, represents the conflicting nature of his views.

Published as the title story in an 1888 volume called *The Happy Prince*, the story was accompanied by the tales "The Nightingale and the Rose," "The Selfish Giant," "The Devoted Friend," and "The Remarkable Rocket." Such fairy tales show the dual influence of two of his most beloved professors and mentors from his days at Oxford University, Walter Pater and John Ruskin. From Ruskin, Wilde learned that art should communicate an understanding or a truth; from Pater, he learned that it need only be beautiful. In his popular fairy tales, Wilde combines both ideas to create a new aesthetic: an art that is both beautiful and instructive.

Although his stance as an aesthete would seem to hinder his ability to write moral tales for children, the father in Wilde could not resist the medium. Fairy tales were immensely popular throughout the 1800s, as the success of Hans Christian Andersen and the Brothers Grimm proved, but Wilde had a more intellectual bent and was interested in reaching a wider audience with his work. He did not intend for his fairy tales to be solely for children, but he utilized a form that would appeal to them nonetheless. Parents who read the stories to their children would do so because they recognized Wilde's name, and children who read them on their own would be subtly exposed to the tenets of aestheticism. A fairy tale was no mere fantasy story in the hands of Oscar Wilde.

"The Happy Prince" is structured like many other fairy tales, containing a setting that is in the past, fantastical elements such as talking animals (and statues), a clear definition between good and evil, a plot centered on a problem that needs to be solved, a resolution, and a moral lesson. However, the main character is a beautiful object of art, the end-

Snow White and the Seven Dwarfs is a well-known fairy tale

ing is not necessarily a "happy" one, and the overarching moral lesson is not as simple as the reader may initially perceive. For, even though the tale ends with God rewarding the good deeds of the Swallow and the Prince, the moral of being kind to others is not Wilde's true lesson. Rather, Wilde is more interested in promoting the "usefulness" of beauty. Art is useful only when it is beautiful and inspiring; that which is not beautiful is not art and should not be displayed as such. When the Art

Professor declares that the shabby Prince "'is no longer beautiful, he is no longer useful,'" Wilde delivers his aesthetic moral lesson (19).

Like the Town Councillor who proclaims that the statue of the Happy Prince is "'as beautiful as a weathercock, . . . only not quite so useful,'" Wilde also "wished to gain a reputation for having artistic tastes" and practical sense (5). In his own life, the author strove to combine his love of beauty with his love of intellect, but, through the quarreling and pretentious Town Councillors, he pokes fun at people who were less than artful in expressing their views on beauty and art. The little Swallow, not the Councillors, is the spokesperson for art and aestheticism. Like the aesthetes, the Swallow possesses an eye for beauty, an appreciation of art, and a taste for the exotic. When he spies the shiny statue of the Happy Prince and shelters himself there, the Swallow is in awe of his "golden bedroom" (7), and in his conversations with the Prince, the bird relates to him the enticing details of Egypt's beautiful sights.

The Prince, though, has no need of such material beauty or exciting travels and stands in direct opposition to the Swallow's pure aestheticism: "'Dear little Swallow,' said the Prince, 'you tell me of marvelous things, but more marvelous than anything is the suffering of men and of women. There is no Mystery so great as Misery'" (16–17). The Prince speaks the truth, and the Swallow realizes it at last. With his two main characters, Wilde sets the theories of his former mentors Walter Pater and John Ruskin side by side and has them work together for good. In doing so, he shows that the most beautiful artwork is not an object—it is a life lived with love.

ABOUT THE AUTHOR

Oscar Wilde was born October 16, 1854, in Dublin, Ireland. Dr. William Wilde, his father, was an internationally known ear and eye surgeon who was outlandishly unfaithful to his wife, Jane Wilde. Before she married William, Jane had passions of her own, such as fighting (on paper) to establish the independence of her beloved Ireland from England's rule in the 1840s. But by the time Oscar was born, she had redefined her role to suit the image of a proper doctor's wife, turning her literary interests to the collection of Irish folklore and establishing a salon, or gathering place, for writers and thinkers of the day. Oscar was exposed at an early age to the adult world of intelligent conversation, and his parents never barred

Oscar Wilde

Oscar or his older brother Willie from mature matters. Perhaps due to the sophisticated environment in which he grew up, Oscar had a distinguished school career that led him to pursue his studies at Oxford University in 1874.

While at Oxford, Wilde adopted the philosophies of two influential professors: art critic John Ruskin and literary critic Walter Pater; Ruskin gave Wilde a social conscience, and Pater gave him a model for his later prose style; both encouraged him to revolt against the constraints of the Victorian era and its official "tastes" in literature and the arts. Wilde followed their advice and wholeheartedly embraced the aesthetic movement. When he graduated from Oxford and set out for London in 1878, he told a friend assuredly, "I'll be a poet, a writer, a dramatist. Somehow or other I'll be famous, and if not famous, I'll be notorious."

Within a few months, Wilde had achieved his goal of becoming a celebrity—even though he had no profession as yet. He did it, primarily, by dressing the part: his strange, eye-catching clothes proclaimed his status as an artist, and his flamboyant self-promotion convinced people that he was a true aesthete. He advertised himself at parties and events within popular artistic circles and made certain he was seen with all the "right" people. As one biographer noted, "Perhaps the most unusual aspect of Wilde's career is the way in which he was able to establish himself as a public figure through force of personality." It certainly was not through his writing at first.

In 1881, Wilde published his first book, a poetry collection simply called *Poems*, which sold well not because of the author's poetic skill but because of his personal popularity. Wilde continued his pattern of promoting himself as a celebrity by associating with other notable artists when he journeyed to the United States in 1882 for a six-month lecture tour that spanned the entire country and made "Oscar Wilde" a household name. Wilde's next undertaking was not a success, though, as he wrote two plays in 1883 that proved to be disasters. Undeterred, he returned to lecturing and married a beautiful and wealthy Irish woman named Constance Lloyd in 1884. The couple soon had two sons, and Wilde became an affectionate father.

In the early years of their marriage, Wilde was dependent upon his wife's money, a situation he remedied in 1887 by becoming the editor of a London magazine called *The Lady's World*. Wilde took the paltry publication to new heights, first by modernizing its title to *The Woman's World* and then by focusing its contents on articles that would appeal to "women of intellect." While editing the magazine, Wilde also published his first book that was a genuine success, a collection of fairy tales called *The Happy Prince*, in 1888. After Wilde left the magazine in 1889, his literary career finally took flight with *The Picture of Dorian Gray* (1891) and three other novels within the next two years. The young author had neared his peak, though. Despite writing his two best plays, *An Ideal Husband* and *The Importance of Being Earnest*, in the mid-1890s, Wilde's life was to be turned upside down by personal turmoil.

In 1891, the 37-year-old Wilde met a charming, handsome young man named Lord Alfred Douglas, and the two formed more than simply a friendship. A few years prior to their meeting, Wilde had begun to experiment with homosexual behavior—which was considered dangerous and criminal in his day—and it led to his arrest and imprisonment in April 1895. The first trial against him ended in a hung jury, but the second trial found him guilty "of extensive corruption of the most hideous kind,"

Oscar Wilde, pictured in 1882

according to the ruling judge. Wilde's companion, Lord Douglas—perhaps because his family was one of the most powerful in the country—was never charged, while Wilde's reputation rapidly disintegrated. He was sentenced to serve two years in prison with hard labor, but what was worse for the writer was that his works stopped selling, and he went bankrupt within a few weeks. Three years after being released from prison, Wilde died of an infectious brain disease on November 30, 1900, in a lonely hotel in Paris.

Published by Creative Education

P.O. Box 227, Mankato, Minnesota 56002

Creative Education is an imprint of The Creative Company.

Design by Rita Marshall; production by Heidi Thompson

Page 21–31 text by Kate Riggs

Printed in the United States of America

Photographs by Corbis (Blue Lantern Studio), Getty Images (Hulton Archive)

Copyright © 2008 Creative Education

Illustrations © 2008 Etienne Delessert

Library of Congress Cataloging-in-Publication Data

Wilde, Oscar, 1854–1900.

The Happy Prince/ by Oscar Wilde.

p. cm. – (Creative short stories)

ISBN 978-1-58341-582-5

I. Title. II. Series.

PR5818.H2 2007

823'.914–dc22   2007008485

First edition

2 4 6 8 9 7 5 3 1